by

Jim Willoughby
and
Sue Willoughby

**GOLDEN
WEST ☼
PUBLISHERS**

Cover design and art by Jim Willoughby

Library of Congress Cataloging-in-Publication Data
Willoughby, Jim.
        Cactus Country: a friendly introduction to cactus of
    the southwest deserts / by Jim and Sue Willoughby.
            p.   cm.
        ISBN 0-914846-71-X
        1. Cactus - - Southwest, New.
        2. Desert plants - - Southwest, New.
        I. Willoughby Sue,   II. Title
    QK495.C11W56   1992
    583' .47'09791 - - dc20   92-44836
                                                        CIP

NOTE: Laws on harvesting native desert plants vary by
state. Before harvesting any native plants, contact your local
state agency.

Printed in the United States of America

ISBN # 0-914846-71-X

Golden West Publishers
4113 N. Longview Ave.
Phoenix, AZ 85014, USA
(602) 265-4392

Foreword

In 1867 a homesick army private wrote from Arizona's Fort Grant to his father in upstate New York, complaining that "there is nothing that grows [here] but what has Prickers." A century later, Arizona Highways photographer Esther Henderson recalled her father gluing paper-and-wax flowers on a saguaro cactus in September (the plant blooms in spring) so that she could fill a calendar company's rush order. The two very different experiences suggest that in nature, as in life generally, truth and beauty often reside in the eyes of the beholder. They also remind us that nothing more clearly conjures up an image of the southwestern desert than the remarkable cactus in all its prickly guises.

Even the tenderest tenderfoot can distinguish a saguaro from a prickly pear. But beyond the obvious, how much do any of us really know about our thorny neighbors? That thought occurred to Prescottonians Jim and Sue Willoughby, and they decided to do something about it. After careful study and a few good chuckles, they have written this entertaining and informative introduction to the amazing cactus. They describe how the plant has adapted to its waterless environment, its important place in the fragile desert ecosystem, and even how some of the larger varieties serve as housing projects for birds and insects. They also show us how to tell a Teddy Bear Cholla (*Opuntia bigelovii*) from a Pancake Prickly Pear (*Opuntia chlorotica*), or an Organ Pipe from a Saguaro. But not every spiny plant is a cactus. The ocotillo, for example, is a member of the Candlewood family. The Willoughbys clear up the confusion when they take a look at the barbed impostors that are commonly mistaken for cactus. Finally, Jim Willoughby's rollicking drawings will bring a smile to the parched lips of even the most desiccated desert rat.

So, sit back and prepare yourself for a treat. In no time at all, you will be amazing friends back east with your knowledge of *Cereus gigantea* and *Echinocereus triglochidiatus*, not to mention *Echinocereus fendleri* and *Mammillaria lasiacantha*. And when you have finished, the desert will be a much friendlier place because you have met some of its most fascinating denizens.

BRUCE J. DINGES
Editor of Publications
Arizona Historical Society

Acknowledgment

We are grateful to Dr. Frank Crosswhite, Curator of Botany at Boyce-Thompson Southwestern Arboretum in Superior, Arizona, for taking his precious personal time to read and comment on the manuscript for this book. He assisted us in simplifying and clarifying vital information, corrected us on significant technical matters, and contributed valuable suggestions we have subsequently incorporated into our text.

Dedication

To our mothers, Edna and Fay. To our granddaughters, Jacqueline and Heather. And to all you cactus lovers out there in Readerland. This is your book.

The Southwest Deserts

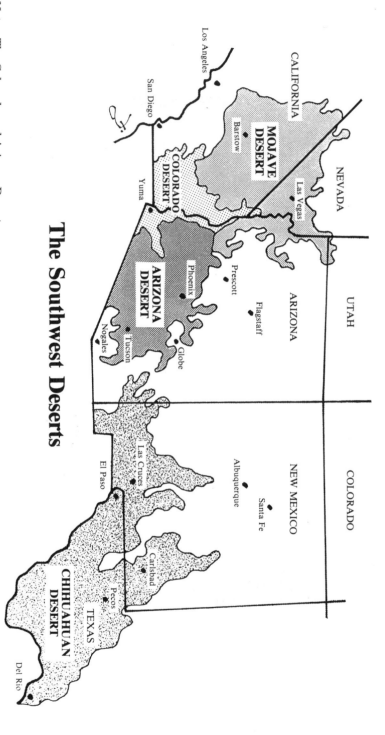

Note: The Colorado and Arizona Deserts are part of the Sonoran Desert.

Contents

Preface

Various cactus species have outstanding characteristics which make them easy to identify. Nearly everyone living in the Southwest knows the classic Saguaro when they see one. The same goes for the jaunty Prickly Pear and cuddly-looking but devastating Teddy Bear Cholla. A few may be able to tell you, "There's a Hedgehog," and you glance about expecting to see a quilled little critter dash by. Beyond the above better known examples, to the average person, cactus is cactus. To the average person, a lot of non-cactus is cactus. Some folks wouldn't know a barrel cactus from a keg of nails.

NOT ME, DUMMY!

OVER HERE!

We presume you to be cactus lovers like ourselves or you wouldn't have picked up this book. Our intent is to share with you some of the things we have learned about these varied denizens of the desert; to acquaint you with some of the more common types of cacti and to show you how to tell one from another. We have also included several plants frequently mistaken for cacti.

Now, when the relatives visit from back east, you'll be able to point out a cactus to them and say, "Yo! By gosh, there's a Corkseed Pincushion." Or better yet, "Would you believe it? Look at that *Mammillaria lasiacantha!*"

Introduction

Cactus. The word stems from the Greek word "kaktos" meaning, literally, "prickly plant." You can't argue with that.

Cacti are part of a group of rugged plants called "succulents" meaning "juicy." All cacti are succulents, though not all succulents are cacti.

GO WATCH WHAT YOU CALL ME, PARDNER!

Indigenous to the Western Hemisphere, cacti (plural for cactus) exist in the Americas from remote regions of Alaska and Canada clear down to the tip of South America. Scientists have placed the beginning of their evolution as a drought-tolerant plant group at upwards to 65 million years ago. As time goes by, more is learned about them and information is updated.

Of the more than 2000 species of cacti, some one hundred make their home in the deserts of the Southwest. This is the region we will deal with here.

Way back in time prolonged drought conditions resulted in large masses of deserts on our continent. As a consequence, many water-dependent plants passed into oblivion. Other more hardy, determined groups managed to adapt and survive by becoming drought resistant. Over time, they replaced their water-hungry leaves with spines and the stems took over the photosynthetic function the leaves previously had accomplished. In essence, they have become the camels of the plant world.

One drawback soon became evident. The deserts were overrun with hunger-ravished, plant-loving animals (herbivorous!) to whom these delectable fleshy plants held considerable appeal. Troubled times for our evolving cactus friends. But, forever adaptable and determined to endure, they reached up their evolutionary sleeve and pulled forth another ace. They developed sharp spines of varying nature, which produced the needed deterrent effect on the heretofore herbivores.

The means for determining what constitutes a true cactus as opposed to other succulents is complex, precise, and pseudo-scientific. Other than for the advisable inclusion of proper Latin names, we have avoided complexities as much as possible.

With the help of drawings and understandable text, you will become acquainted with some of the more outstanding cacti found in the southwestern deserts of the United States. These include the vast expanses of the Mojave, Sonoran and Chihuahuan Deserts, which extend from Southern California across southern Nevada and Utah, Arizona and New Mexico into west Texas.

The book is set up in major group classifications of southwest cacti, followed with several key species representative of each group. You will learn there is more than one type of Prickly Pear, for instance, and an abundance of Cholla (choy-ya) and Hedgehogs, to mention just a few.

Cactus Anatomy

Stem—The stem may be said to be the body of a cactus. It is manifested in a great variety of sizes and shapes and may occur branched or unbranched.

Tubercle—Tubercles are protrusions along the stems of certain cacti such as Cholla. At their tops, they produce areoles.

Areole—Areoles consist of an upper and lower bud tightly joined and occur spirally along a stem or at the tops of tubercles. The upper buds produce flowers and fruits while the lower bear the spine arrangements.

Spine—Spines are sharp, sometimes barbed, projections from areoles. They serve the cactus as protective devices and are best appreciated when not attached to your epidermis!

Glochid—Pronounced "glokid," these tiny, sharp-pointed and barbed bristles appear in small clusters, just above the regular spine cluster and are found only among the Prickly Pears and Chollas. They are hard to see and tough to remove, so are worth the effort to avoid.

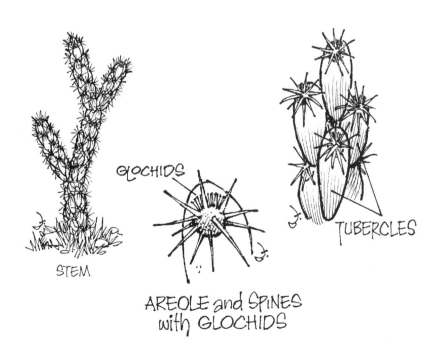

STEM

GLOCHIDS

AREOLE and SPINES
with GLOCHIDS

TUBERCLES

OPUNTIA

PRICKLY PEARS and CHOLLAS

The Opuntia cacti are comprised of series of joints, each from another, and are without ribs. Prickly Pear joints appear in the form of pads: fleshy, flat and leaf-like. Cholla joints are oval to cylindrical with elongated tubercles and are sharply barbed. Their spines are covered with papery material. Flowers and fruits grow from the preceding season's joints near their apex and within spine-bearing areoles. The fruits are fleshy and edible provided you carefully remove the glochids and peel them first.

Young prickly pear pads are called "nopalito" in Mexico where they are prepared and eaten as vegetables. Javelina like the pads also. They eat them, spines and ALL, and dig for the roots as well, which they devour with much gusto.

PRICKLY PEARS:

Beavertail

Brown-spined Prickly Pear

Purple Prickly Pear

Engelmann's Prickly Pear

Pancake Prickly Pear

CHOLLAS:

Buckhorn Cholla

Cane Cholla

Staghorn Cholla

Jumping Cholla

Teddy Bear Cholla

"I can't get a word out of this earthling!"

PRICKLY PEAR

BEAVERTAIL
(Opuntia basilaris)

The velvet-textured pads of this bluish-gray cactus are 1/2" thick and round to elongated, resembling a beaver's tail. They have no spines, but abound in groups of inglorious glochids. Branching from the lower parts of older pads, the Beavertail forms clumps close to the ground. In early April, large magenta to deep-rose flowers pop forth in abundance. These are succeeded by green to gray, dry, spineless fruits.

Beavertail prospers in sandy, gravelly soil to a 4000-foot elevation in the deserts of southern California, Nevada, Utah and western Arizona.

BEAVERTAIL

BROWN-SPINED PRICKLY PEAR
(Opuntia phaeacantha, variety major)

This most common of all the southwest Prickly Pears grows prostrate with no trunk. It sends out chains of blue-green pads along the ground, forming large clumps three feet high to twenty feet around. These oblong pads sometimes part company with the mother plant and take root on contact with the soil underneath. Far-separated clusters of long, flattened spines are red-brown, unbarbed and are more dense toward the tops of pads. The abundant flowers are large and yellow, giving way to red-purple fruit, which is fleshy and smooth.

They are found in medium to high elevation juniper and pinyon woodlands in Arizona, Utah, Colorado, northern New Mexico and parts of Texas.

BROWN-SPINED PRICKLY PEAR

PURPLE PRICKLY PEAR
(Opuntia violacea)

Featuring a short trunk, this prickly prince grows like a sprawling shrub to seven feet high, somewhat like a small tree. Its pads are green to blue-purple, 3/8" thick and oblong in shape. Long, dark colored spines grow singularly at right angles to the upper parts of the pads. The numerous yellow flowers sport red centers. The red to red-purple fruit is fleshy and smooth.

This species is found in upper-desert hills, mesas and canyons in southeast Arizona and southwest New Mexico.

PURPLE PRICKLY PEAR

"... and a shot of water for
my dry friend here!"

ENGELMANN'S PRICKLY PEAR
(Opuntia phaeacantha, variety discata)

This is one of the more common Prickly Pears. Trunkless, it spreads widely and reaches heights of five feet. Its oblong, thin green pads are among the largest of all native U.S. Prickly Pears. Its areoles bulge from the pads and are widespread. Large, lemon-yellow flowers are replaced eventually by big, juicy fruits loaded with glochids. Take away the glochids and peel the fruit for a tasty treat.

You'll find it prospering from the desert floor up onto mountainsides in southern California, western to southeastern Arizona, New Mexico and in west Texas.

ENGELMANN'S PRICKLY PEAR

Peeling a Prickly Pear

PANCAKE PRICKLY PEAR
(Opuntia chlorotica)

This unique blue-green cactus grows upright to six feet high and four feet in diameter. Shrub-like in appearance, it has a thick, round trunk and normally clings to the sandy, rocky soils of steep ledges and mountain slopes. There is a single, unexplained exception. In one flat desert location a few miles north of Wickenburg, Arizona, near Congress and Aguila, there exists a vast stand of Pancake Prickly Pear, good-looking to view and appearing to be larger than those found in other locations.

A profusion of circular six to seven-inch bluish pads on the Pancake Prickly Pear have widely separated areoles which are full of yellow glochid clusters. As many as five longer golden spines point down from each areole. Broad yellow flowers precede purplish-green, pear-shaped fruits.

The Pancake flourishes to a 6000-foot elevation in southern California and Nevada, across Arizona into southeastern New Mexico.

PANCAKE PRICKLY PEAR

"Try more syrup on it!"

CHOLLA

BUCKHORN CHOLLA
(Opuntia acanthocarpa)

Depending on its location, this Cholla grows as a shrub or small tree. It may get to be ten feet tall. Straggly dark green woody branches, 1 1/2" in diameter, alternate upward and out from its short trunk. Elongated, flattened tubercles protrude lengthwise along the stems and bear many yellowish glochids with seven to twenty spines per areole. The light-colored spines are sheathed and of differing lengths. They cross over each other erratically giving the Buckhorn its shaggy look. The good-sized flowers bloom in April and May, ranging in color from light yellow to orange, pink and red. The fruits are dry and tubular with numerous spreading spines.

The Buckhorn grows to a 4000-foot elevation in southern California, southern Nevada, southwest Utah and Arizona.

BUCKHORN CHOLLA

CANE CHOLLA
(Opuntia spinosior)

This frost-tolerant cactus grows as a shrub or small tree. From a substantial short trunk, its thick, tubular branches extend upward to eight feet in a haphazard manner. It has numerous tubercles and ten to twenty short, sheathed spines per areole, spreading in all directions. Its two-inch flowers are purple and red to yellow. The lemon-yellow fruits are fleshy, tubular and smooth.

Canes, lamp bases and other craft items are created from its attractive, interlaced woody skeleton.

It is found in the desert and in the higher mountain grasslands and juniper stands in Arizona and southwestern New Mexico where other Chollas don't thrive.

DETAIL

CANE CHOLLA

STAGHORN CHOLLA
(Opuntia versicolor)

The Staghorn grows to 18 feet as a small tree with a short trunk. Its dull-green branches are long and slender with prominent tubercles. Many short, sheathed spines spread every which way. They are red, gray or yellow and not strongly barbed. Medium-sized flowers abound in a wide array of colors, thus the name "versicolor." Numerous fruits are smooth and form short "chains."

This ragged but handsome specimen is found up to a 3000-foot elevation in the deserts and mountains of southern Arizona. Look for it in Tucson's foothills.

STAGHORN CHOLLA

JUMPING CHOLLA
(Opuntia fulgida)

This attractive but formidable cactus grows into a small tree, reaching heights of 15 feet. It groups in flat desert regions to form virtual forests. Its trunk will reach three feet to the first branches. The branches are generally longer than the trunk and branch and rebranch. The joints are cylindrical to six inches in length and two inches in diameter. They detach without much urging and either grab onto your trouser legs or fall on the ground to root and form new plants. This is its main means of reproduction. Its dense spines are straw-colored, long and sheathed, and tend to obscure the stem. They are barbed and don't pull out of your leg easily. The exceptionally attractive flowers are small, white to pink, with streaks of lavender. The green fruits are small, smooth and fleshy. They form long "chains" and are often called "Chain-fruit Chollas."

This cactus is at home in southern Arizona, up to 3000 feet.

JUMPING CHOLLA

"I've been pruning the cholla!"

TEDDY BEAR CHOLLA
(Opuntia bigelovii)

This attractive specimen with its teddy bear resemblance takes the form of a small three foot to nine foot tree. Its trunk extends the full height and appears black as its spines darken. The green joints are short and elliptical. They detach readily and by falling to the ground and taking root, produce new plants. Packrats gather them presumably for their protective qualities to use in the construction of their nests. Dense, flat and heavily-barbed spines obscure the stems. They are nasty to remove from your skin, so avoid them. The smallish flowers are pale green or yellow streaked with lavender. The yellow fruits are fleshy and strongly tubercled.

The Teddy Bear is abundant in the desert regions of southern California and Nevada, and in northwestern to southern Arizona.

TEDDY BEAR CHOLLA

"Gotcha!"

CEREUS

Cereus cacti are one of the more common and better known genera. They are found in drier desert regions and are comprised of long stems with surface ridges and grooves. Always ribbed, many are night bloomers, usually with white or pale-colored flowers to attract nocturnal pollinators. For the same reason, they are attractively fragrant. Flowers grow from the sides of the stems or just below the tips.

SAGUARO

ORGAN PIPE

SENITA

NIGHT-BLOOMING CEREUS

SAGUARO

SAGUARO
(Cereus gigantea)

These huge specimens are the condors of the desert, soaring high above all else around them. Initially slow growing, they reach heights in excess of fifty feet and often live to be more than two hundred years old.

Saguaro are picturesque with their multiple, often weirdly twisted branches. Though found mainly in the southern regions of Arizona, they cross over into parts of California and down into Old Mexico.

They like rocky, gravelly soil, and thrive along south-facing slopes and foothills at elevations to 3500 feet, becoming veritable landmarks in some places. They bloom in May and June with attractive circles of flowers at the ends of their branches. Egg-shaped fruits develop in June and July and Native Americans eat them just as they are, sans spines, or make them into a delicious jelly and candy, or ferment them into a mild tasty wine. The Saguaro has a skeleton of long, hard woody ribs which some Indian and Mexican peoples use in roof and hacienda construction. Lizards find hiding places in their otherwise inhospitable crevices, and hawks, vultures, crows and other birds build comfortable nests where the Saguaro branches join their trunks. Woodpeckers peck holes in their sides and hollow out neat little chambers in which to raise a woodpecker family. When the woodpecker inevitably vacates, elf owls, cactus wrens or other small birds take up residence.

An excellent place to see outstanding Saguaro specimens is the Saguaro National Monument, fourteen miles east of Tucson.

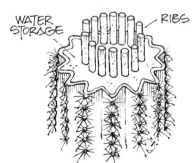

Saguaro Section
Detail

ORGAN PIPE
(Cereus thurberi)

These are big plants with many slender, columnar branches curving upward to as high as twenty feet from a central point at ground level. The visual effect is that of a musical organ. Their rounded ribs are deep green in color and feature dense, dark gray, needle-like spines, with as many as nineteen per areole. Small white to pale lavender flowers sprout at night. They remain open only through the next day so those little moths which pollinate them have to hustle to get their job done. Native Americans utilize the fruit in much the same way they use the Saguaro fruit.

The Organ Pipe is found in desert valleys and on rocky south-facing hills and mesas in the deserts of Arizona and New Mexico. Splendid examples may be seen in the Organ Pipe National Monument in southern Arizona.

HEY, MAN, WHERE'S THE KEYBOARD?

ORGAN PIPE

SENITA
(Lophocereus schotti)

This multiple-branched cactus reaches to twenty-one feet high. Its sturdy, light green stems grow out and up from the base. They are sharp- angled with five to nine prominent ribs per stem. Adults will sport thirty to fifty long, flattened, bristly gray spines protruding from each areole, giving it the appearance of an old senile person, hence the name.

The small, light pink flowers occur with more than one per areole, rare among cacti. They bloom at night and emit an unpleasant smell, though the moths which pollinate them don't seem to mind. They get the job done. The fruit is red, fleshy, globular to oval shaped, and ripens in the fall.

Senita is found in desert valleys and plains under a 1500-foot elevation, thriving particularly well around the Organ Pipe National Monument in Pima County, Arizona.

Senita Detail

SENITA

NIGHT-BLOOMING CEREUS
(Cereus greggii)

Also referred to as "Queen of the Night," this is a classy, peculiar little item and hard to find. It grows under desert shrubs and small trees, using them for shade and to support its slender, grayish-blue stems. These stems have four to six ribs with many tiny, black inconsequential spines along them. They are generally 1/2" in diameter and may grow to eight feet in length, rising from a single, dead-looking woody base.

Called "Sweet Potato" by some, its food resources are stored underground in large, turnip-shaped tubers which sometimes grow to one hundred pounds. These tubers are edible and relished by anyone lucky enough to locate them, as well as by birds and desert rodents.

We are informed by Dr. Frank Crosswhite that the Apaches use this tuber as an ingredient in their "tulapai," an intoxicating drink they create. He observes that it may have a bit more kick than a turnip and hopes our readers won't try to make a salad from one.

Large, beautiful white flowers open after dark in June or early July and emit a tantalizing perfumy smell which carries a considerable distance. This inspires the name, "Queen of the Night." The flowers close with the arrival of morning. The fruit which follows is large, red and tasty to birds and rodents.

This prize thrives in alluvial bottomlands and hillsides in central and southern Arizona, across southern New Mexico and into west Texas.

Night-Blooming
Cereus Flower
Detail

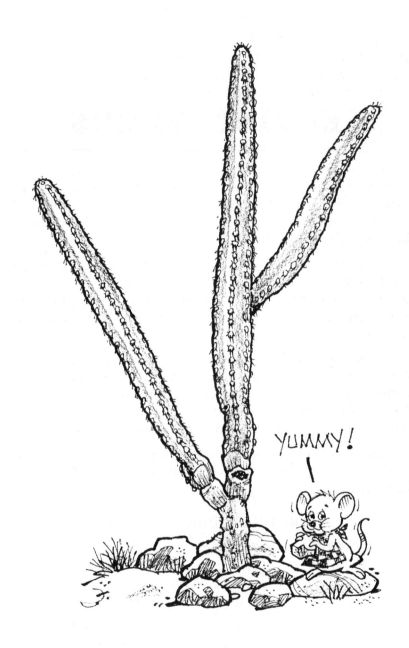

NIGHT-BLOOMING CEREUS

ECHINOCEREUS

This group is made up of the various cacti called Hedgehog. They are relatively short-stemmed, always ribbed and with surface ridges and grooves. While occasionally single-stemmed, their stems tend more to branch from the base and form clumps or large mounds. They like full sun when they can get it. Showy flowers appear above the areoles in the upper parts of the stems. The fruit is edible once care is taken to first remove the many spines.

CLARET CUP

LEDING'S HEDGEHOG

FENDLERS HEDGEHOG

ROBUST HEDGEHOG

STRAWBERRY HEDGEHOG

ARIZONA RAINBOW CACTUS

CLARET CUP
(Echinocereus triglochidiatus)

The Claret Cup is one of the numerous Hedgehog species. Its blue-green cylindrical stems are ribbed and grow as long as 14". The areoles along the ribs each bear eight to sixteen sharp spines.

Tightly grouped, as many as 500 stems will mass into a dense mound a foot high and four feet across. They are found in abundance across the Southwest and vary astoundingly in appearance. Their many round-petaled flowers bloom in April and May. This is the only Hedgehog in the United States to bear red flowers. The red fruit is delectably juicy and edible.

This species likes the granite soils of hillsides and canyons and is found bordering the deserts of southern California, Nevada, Utah and Arizona. Varieties may be found, too, in southern Colorado and down through New Mexico into west Texas.

CLARET CUP

"Hey, dig the Echinocereus triglochidiatus!"

LEDING'S HEDGEHOG
(Echinocereus ledingii)

This large Hedgehog grows in small clumps consisting of four to ten stems to a clump. Its cylindrical, light green stems are 1 1/2 to 3" in diameter and up to 20" in length. There are 12 to 16 ribs per stem with yellow to straw-colored spines along their length. The principal spines are 1" long, needle-like and turn downward, partially hiding the stem. Its large flowers are magenta to rose-purple in color and the fruit is green, turning to red.

This cactus likes the gravelly slopes of mountains in southeast Arizona, especially the Pinaleno Mountains in Graham County.

LEDING'S HEDGEHOG

FENDLER'S HEDGEHOG
(Echinocereus fendleri)

This cactus occasionally branches close to the ground with four or five stems resulting. More often though, it grows singular to 10" high with a green ribbed stem that is oval to cylindrical in shape and as much as 2 1/2" in diameter. Tubercles protrude along the ribs with short white spines punctuated by a more prominent outward-pointing dark central spine. The gorgeous flowers are as large as 2 1/2" in diameter and magenta colored, followed by a green fruit which turns eventually to red.

You'll find this prize in higher elevation grasslands tucked amongst oaks, junipers and pinyon pines in eastern Arizona and western New Mexico.

FENDLER'S HEDGEHOG

HEDGEHOG

ROBUST HEDGEHOG
(Echinocereus fasciculatus)

The green stems of this cactus often reach a height of 18" and occur in small clumps of from three to twenty stems per clump. They are firm and cylindrical, up to 3" in diameter, with an average of ten ribs to the stem. The overall look is one of robustness, providing its name.

A principal, needle-like central spine turns downward and is attended by one or two equally needle-like but shorter secondary centrals. In addition are a dozen or so spreading radial spines of differing lengths which give the Robust a decidedly shaggy look. Its magenta to reddish-purple flowers are big and decorative. The fruit is green turning to red and good eating.

It will be found in central and southern Arizona over into southern New Mexico.

ROBUST HEDGEHOG

STRAWBERRY HEDGEHOG
(Echinocereus engelmannii)

Fifty to sixty stems of this cactus will be found together forming large impressive mounds as much as a foot high. These stems are green and cylindrical with occasionally a dozen tubercled ribs bearing many spines close to the stems. There are several central spines, one of which is flattened, 1 1/2" long and much like a sword in appearance.

The prolific flowers and fruits are similar to those of the Robust Hedgehog. The fruits contain lots of sugar and are often harvested for their tastiness.

This cactus is found up to a 5000-foot elevation in the deserts of southern California, southern Nevada and in south-central Arizona. Numerous striking specimens show their stuff in Organ Pipe National Monument.

STRAWBERRY HEDGEHOG

ARIZONA RAINBOW CACTUS
(Echinocereus rigidissimus)

Providing it protection from the sun, numerous crowded areoles of many short, colorful radial spines lie flat against this beauty's stem to create alternating color bands along its length. These colors range from white to cream, pink and red, inspiring the name "Rainbow." Always a beauty, the Arizona Rainbow grows alone and erect to 14" high in the shape of a flattened cylinder. Because of its flattened spines, it can be handled without sticking the handler. Its large flowers are red to purple with a white throat. The fruit is green and spiny.

This Rainbow likes the limestone hills and grasslands of southern Arizona and southwest New Mexico, ranging down into Old Mexico.

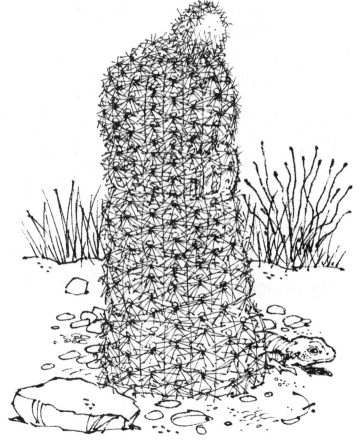

ARIZONA RAINBOW CACTUS

MAMMILLARIA

PINCUSHIONS and FISHHOOKS

These are stemmed cacti that range from 1" to 12" tall and up to 8" in diameter, with separate tubercles. Usually single-stemmed, they occasionally branch and are grouped into species with straight spines (pincushion) or with hook-tipped central spines (fishhook). The spines are smooth and of a broad color range. Flowers are produced in rings around the stem between older tubercles and are replaced by fleshy, spineless fruit.

The chile-shaped red fruits of small pincushion cacti are called "chillitos" in the Southwest. They have a sharp strawberry taste.

PINCUSHIONS:

       Cream Pincushion
       Golf Ball Pincushion
       Corkseed Pincushion
       Clustered Pincushion

FISHHOOKS:

       Arizona Golden Fishhook
       Big-fruited Fishhook

"You aren't supposed to pet it!"

CREAM PINCUSHION
(Mammillaria macdougalii)

A lone cactus usually growing flat on the ground, this handsome species takes on a rounder shape as it gets older. It grows to eight inches in diameter and features a carrot-shaped root. Dense spines grow from flat tubercles without hiding the stem. Short radial spines lie parallel to the stem with two 3/8" brown centrals extending at right angles from the stem. Small late spring flowers, pink to white or cream, form a ring around the center of the cactus. The red fruit which develops is fleshy and edible.

This Pincushion likes full sun and lots of rain. It is found at higher elevations on hillsides and in mountain valleys in southern Arizona and across New Mexico into west Texas.

CREAM PINCUSHION

GOLF BALL PINCUSHION
(Mammillaria lasiacantha)

Small and usually solitary, this globular cactus protrudes slightly above the ground surface and has the appearance of a golf ball. Numerous tiny tubercles contain clusters of small, white, bristly spines which interlace and lie flat to hide the surface of the stem, permitting it to be handled without the handler getting stuck. The small flowers are white with a red mid-stripe. The fruit is long, narrow and fleshy.

This cactus likes rocky, limestone hills and mesas in desert and grassland areas up to a 4300-foot elevation. It finds these conditions in Cochise County, Arizona, southern New Mexico and along the Pecos River in west Texas.

GOLF BALL PINCUSHION

CORKSEED PINCUSHION
(Mammillaria tetrancistra)

Seeing one of these cacti somewhere is no assurance you will find another nearby. They grow at considerable distances from each other in drier parts of the desert. Single-stemmed, three to six inches high and 2 1/2 inches in diameter, they don't like much moisture. Many 1/2" white radial spines per tubercle obscure the cactus entirely. Occasionally, these radials are tipped dark red. Up to four red to black central spines per areole, one inch long and hooked, stick out from the plant, giving it a distinctive look. The flowers are large and may range from pink to purple. They occur in June and July, followed by bright red, club-shaped fruits.

This pincushion grows in sandy soils to 2500-foot elevations in southern California, southwest Nevada, southern Utah and western Arizona.

CORKSEED PINCUSHION

*"Otherwise, how was your visit
to the cactus gardens?"*

CLUSTERED PINCUSHION
(Mammillaria thornberi)

The Clustered Pincushion grows a single stem that is narrow relative to its eight to ten-inch height. Multiple single stems will form clumps of up to a hundred stems. They need shade from full sun and tend to prosper under shrubs or taller cacti. The cylindrical green stem tapers gradually down into its root system. Dense short radial spines partially hide the stem. They are white with red-brown tips. One red-brown central spine, 1/2" long and hooked, extends at a right angle to the stem. The lavender flowers are small with few petals. The fruit is red, juicy and edible.

This cactus thrives in fine, sandy soil in Arizona, largely on the Tohono O'odham Indian Reservation.

CLUSTERED PINCUSHION

ARIZONA GOLDEN FISHHOOK
(Mammillaria microcarpa)

This moisture-tolerant beauty is single-stemmed initially and branches as it ages. The stems vary from globular to cylindrical, are about two inches in diameter and up to six inches long. A dense array of pale-colored radial spines occur parallel to the stem, partially obscuring it. One hooked, red to black-purple central spine sticks out at a right angle to the stem. Small, pink flowers circle the plant in June or July and last several days. The cylindrical fruits which result are golden orange and are relished by birds and small desert animals.

This Fishhook likes the shade of desert shrubs and small trees in western, central and southern Arizona.

ARIZONA GOLDEN FISHHOOK

BIG-FRUITED FISHHOOK
(Mammillaria wrightii)

The stem of this jewel is single, green and globular, approximately four inches high by three inches in diameter. Short, white spines are straight and dense, growing parallel to the stem, partially hiding it. Its central spines are few, long, dark and hooked. Wondrous flowers, large and red-purple to magenta, appear in late summer followed by large, grape-shaped fruits.

It is prominent in east-central Arizona and northeast New Mexico.

BIG-FRUITED FISHHOOK

FEROCACTUS

Because of its large stem and barrel shape, this plant has inspired the name "barrel cactus" which, tradition maintains, provides drinking water for thirsty desert travelers. Its pulp can, in fact, be crushed to create an unappetizing liquid, but you'd have to be on the desperate side to imbibe it. Some Ferocactus are quite small. All are ribbed with surface ridges and grooves. They feature heavy radial spines with one or more curved central spines. Native Americans often use these curved centrals to snare fish. Flowers occur near the top of the stem close to the growing point. The fruit is fleshy with scales and isn't widely regarded as gourmet fare.

ARIZONA BARREL

CALIFORNIA BARREL

SONORA BARREL

"I'm hooked on you!"

ARIZONA BARREL
(Ferocactus wislizenii)

This fellow is single-stemmed and massive. Sometimes two feet in diameter and reaching ten feet high, it is occasionally thought to be a young Saguaro. It is fatter, though, and barrel-shaped with sturdy, hooked spines. There are from twenty to twenty-eight ribs in an Arizona Barrel and many radial, white bristle-like spines, 1 3/4" long, along its stem, nearly obscuring it. Four central spines in each areole form something of a cross. The main central spine is long, flat, crossed with ridges and ends in a substantial hook. Large orange, red and sometimes yellow flowers appear in August and September, later than in the case of most cacti. The lemon-yellow fruit is fleshy and scaly. Small animals and rodents love it. The fruit and stem interiors are used in the making of cactus candy, which has resulted in a serious decimation of this cactus in the Southwest.

Found in southern Arizona and southwest New Mexico, the

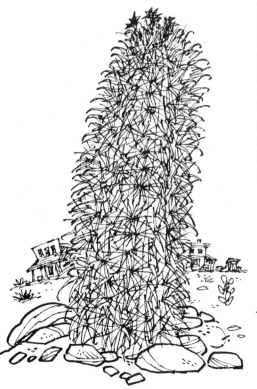

frost-resistant Arizona Barrel likes deep, rocky, gravelly soil. It grows faster on the shady side, so tends to lean to the south, giving desert travelers good cause to refer to it as "Compass Cactus." Sometimes it leans so far as to topple over.

ARIZONA BARREL

"How long you been in Cactus Country, Slim?"

CALIFORNIA BARREL
(Ferocactus acanthodes)

Cylindrical, columnar stems approximately one foot in diameter and six feet high have 18 to 27 ribs and seldom branch. Dense yellow to red radial spines cover the lengthy stem. Ridged central spines, 2 1/2" long, form a cross and are not hooked. Large yellow flowers appear in the spring and early summer following rains. The yellow fruit is fleshy and scaled, much like that of the Arizona Barrel.

Hot desert regions appeal to this specimen as well as hillsides and canyon walls to a 2000-foot elevation. It occurs abundantly in southeast California, southern Nevada, southwest Utah and southern Arizona.

CALIFORNIA BARREL

SONORA BARREL
(Ferocactus covillei)

From a distance, this giant resembles the Arizona Barrel Cactus. The seven or eight-foot tall stem is barrel-shaped and not branched unless it has been injured. There are seven to nine radial spines per areole, deep red except for two white horizontal ones and one central spine, three to four inches long, at a right angle to the stem. It curves downward and is hooked at the end; is red with a flat, ridged upper surface, and a rounded lower surface. The large flowers are maroon or purplish-red. The fruit is yellow and scaled.

This cactus will be found in grassy desert flats, on gravelly, rocky hills and in washes and alluvial fan areas in southern Arizona near the Mexican border. Together with the Arizona and California Barrels, it is abundant on the Pima Indian Reservation and in the Organ Pipe National Monument.

SONORA BARREL

ECHINOCACTUS

Another barrel cactus with branched or un-branched stems growing to two feet long and one foot in diameter. The stem surface is ridged and grooved with up to twenty-seven ribs supporting it. Flowers and fleshy fruit develop near the tops of the stems, as with the Ferocactus.

MANY-HEADED BARREL

BLUE BARREL

MOJAVE PINEAPPLE

"Maybe if I was thinner they wouldn't call me a barrel!"

MANY-HEADED BARREL
(Echinocactus polycephalus)

This multi-headed smaller barrel branches into large mounds of as many as 30 heads to a mound. The stems are spherical to cylindrical, 9" in diameter and up to 24" long, with 13 to 21 ribs per stem. The spines are very dense, obscuring the plant. Radial spines are 1 3/4" long and curve in arcs. Four central spines are 3" long, flattened, ridged and spread randomly. The main one curves downward. The two-inch flowers are yellow and pink with toothed tips. The fruit is dry and covered with matted white hairs 3/4" long.

The Many-headed Barrel can be found on rocky desert slopes to a 2000-foot elevation and in Mojave Desert valleys of southern California, southern Nevada and western Arizona.

MANY-HEADED BARREL

"I feel like we're developing a split personality!"

BLUE BARREL
(Echinocactus horizonthalonius)

Also called Eagle Claws, this small single-stemmed, barrel-shaped cactus grows to six-inches in diameter and up to twelve inches high. It may appear near another of its type, but they don't form mounds. The spines along its flattened ribs are densely situated without obscuring the stem. Its one-inch radial spines curve outward from the areole with three long central spines curving downward. The large flowers appearing at the top of the plant are bright pink, and their base sits in thick, white wool. So do the fruits when they develop. These are dry and covered with the woolly substance.

The Blue Barrel's overall blue-green color blends into limestone environments and makes this cactus tough to locate. It prefers limestone soils and thrives up to an elevation of 5500 feet in south-central Arizona, southwest New Mexico and west Texas.

BLUE BARREL

MOJAVE PINEAPPLE
(Echinocactus johnsonii)

This solitary oval to elliptical cactus grows to ten inches high and, as you guessed, roughly resembles a pineapple in size and shape. Spines are so densely situated that they pretty much hide the plant's four-inch diameter stem. Numerous long, light-colored radial spines back up four to eight 1 1/2" long pink to red centrals. The spines criss-cross each other somewhat and tend to blacken as the plant ages. Large deep-pink flowers appear, followed by green, scaly fruit.

This loner grows in California in the vicinity of Death Valley and in southern Nevada and west-central Arizona up to a 4000-foot elevation.

MOJAVE PINEAPPLE

"I think I prefer Hawaiian Pineapple!"

CORYPHANTHA

PINCUSHION

This is a group of solitary, rounded plants with large, grooved tubercles and sturdy spines. They rarely branch and have no ribs. Large pink or yellow flowers grow at the base of the upper sides of the tubercles at the top of the plant. The fruits are green or yellow, smooth, thin-skinned and juicy. They are oval shaped and about the size of a grape. Stout spines usually do not hide the plant.

GIANT PINCUSHION

GOLDEN PINCUSHION

BISCUIT PINCUSHION

FOXTAIL CACTUS

"Out working in the cactus again?"

GIANT PINCUSHION
(Coryphantha scheeri)

This globular cactus usually grows alone. Occasionally, one will get lonely and be found with others. Its gray-green stem grows to four inches in diameter by nine inches high and takes the shape of a beehive or small barrel cactus. Its prominent tubercles are nearly an inch long and grooved on their upper surface. Dense radial spines spread at the base of several heavy, hooked central spines, which are straw-colored with reddish tips. Its large flowers are yellow with red streaks, succeeded by elliptical, green fruits.

It is found at elevations to 5000 feet in southern Arizona and New Mexico, and on into southwestern Texas.

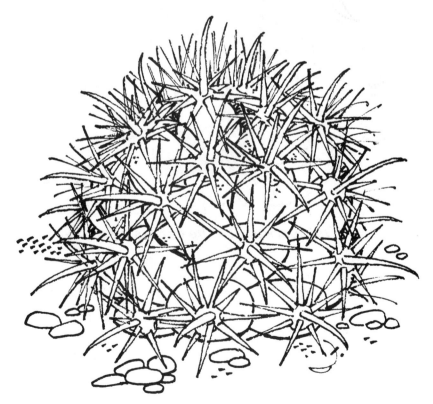

GIANT PINCUSHION

GOLDEN PINCUSHION
(Coryphantha recurvata)

The light green stems of this cactus grow to ten inches high and six inches in diameter. They occur close together in large clumps of as many as fifty stems. Short, yellow radial spines curve slightly and spread parallel to the stem, all but covering it. Single, short, central spines are red-tipped, and curve out and downward giving this pincushion an overall neat look. Its small yellow flowers occur near the top of the plant at irregular intervals. The fruit is green and spherical.

This is a rare cactus found only in Santa Cruz County, Arizona and in nearby Sonora, Mexico.

Golden
Pincushion
Detail

GOLDEN PINCUSHION

BISCUIT PINCUSHION
(Coryphantha vivipara)

A hardy survivor, this sturdy little bundle of spines gets through 9000-foot winters. Its green stems are globular to cylindrical and form wide clumps sometimes a foot high. Dense spines partially cover the stems. Many white radials lie parallel to the stem while several stout and straight centrals point outward. These are usually white and tipped with pink. The flowers are large and open. In some varieties they may flower for only one or two hours of one day. The fruit is green and elliptical to about an inch long.

The Biscuit Pincushion prospers in high desert areas from southern California through Arizona and New Mexico to western Texas.

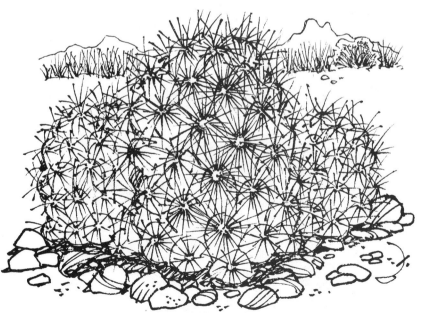

BISCUIT PINCUSHION

FOXTAIL CACTUS
(Coryphantha alversonii)

This cactus is special to us. Our "discovery" of it years ago while on a camping excursion with our children near Twenty-Nine Palms, California, and our subsequent delving for information about it brought us to a broader study of cacti. A handsome plant, cylindrical in shape, it grows to be eight inches high by three inches in diameter and frequently branches at its base. Many black-tipped white radial and central spines cover its body and appear to point in all directions. Its overall appearance is that of a fox's tail. Pink flowers feature pointed petals and the resultant fruit is green.

The Foxtail is primarily found in southeastern California.

FOXTAIL CACTUS

PLANTS SOMETIMES THOUGHT TO BE CACTI

OCOTILLO

JOSHUA TREE

SPANISH BAYONET

BROADLEAF YUCCA

MESCAL or CENTURY PLANT

DESERT AGAVE

AMOLE

SOTOL

"... but I FEEL like a cactus!"

OCOTILLO
(Fouquieria splendens)

Also called "Coachwhip," this relaxed-looking member of the Candlewood family features numerous long, rarely branching stems growing out and up from a common base. These slender green stems are spiny and covered with green, scaly bark. Small, rounded leaves grow in abundance along the stems when it rains, then drop off when the ground dries. This may happen several times in a year. Bright red flowers grow in dense clusters at the tips of the stems in April and May creating a beautiful sight. The stems are sometimes used in building huts or are planted in rows to root and grow into living fences.

The Ocotillo is found widespread in desert regions of southern California, Arizona, New Mexico and Texas.

OCOTILLO

Ocotillo
Detail

JOSHUA TREE
(Yucca brevifolia)

This tree-like member of the Lily family can reach 15 to 35 feet high and spread to 20 feet in diameter. Some have been found to be 60 to 80 feet in height. It has a trunk and many branches with short leaves in dense groups forming a crown. Tight clusters of greenish-white, long bell-shaped flowers grow at the ends of its branches, though not every year. Flowering intervals are determined by temperature and amount of rain, usually from February to April. For thousands of years the Joshua Tree has been pollinated by the grayish-white *Pronuba synthetica* moth in what is called a symbiotic relationship. Each depends on the other for its existence.

The Joshua Tree got its name from Mormons in the 1880s after the biblical Joshua because of its uplifted arms. Some are thought to be 200 to 300 years old, but there are no tree rings to prove it.

"Take my word for it!"

Some California specimens are thought to be much older. Dating back millions of years to the Pliocene Epoch, they once provided food for giant ground sloths and shade for herds of little prehistoric horses and camels.

Today the Joshua Tree shelters and feeds desert birds, lizards, woodrats and several species of insects. The Joshua Tree National Monument near Twenty-Nine Palms in southern California has a particularly fine stand, but it also can be found in abundance throughout the deserts of California, southern Nevada, southwest Utah and northwest Arizona.

JOSHUA TREE

SPANISH BAYONET
(Yucca whipplei)

The Spanish Bayonet is called by some, "Our Lord's Candle." This narrow-leaved plant grows in packed clusters of eight to twelve, with fibers extruding from its leaf margins. Spreading plumes of creamy-white flowers occur at the end of a stout stalk nightly in May and June and appear to glow.

It is found widespread throughout the Southwest.

SPANISH BAYONET

BROADLEAF YUCCA
(Yucca arizonica)

Creamy-colored flowers occur on this broad-leaved Yucca in April and May. They are strongly scented and bell-shaped. The plant grows as high as fifteen feet in good circumstances. Leaf fibers are woven into ropes, sandals, baskets and cloth. Its seeds were ground into meal by early Native Americans, and the buds, flowers, fruits and young stalks became food items. The roots were made into soap.

The Broadleaf Yucca is found mainly in the deserts of southern Arizona.

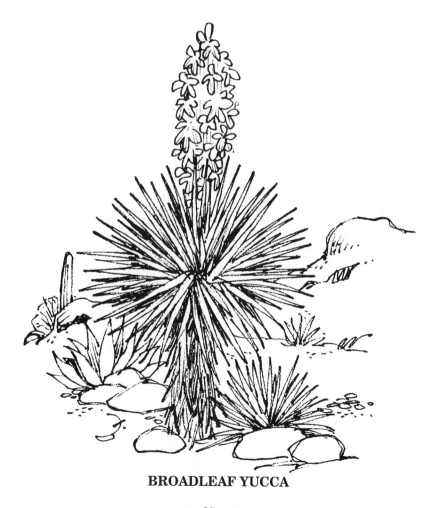

BROADLEAF YUCCA

"It likes you!"

AGAVE

These native Americans are often called Century Plants, though they rarely live longer than 15 or 20 years. They have no trunk. Thick, evergreen, long, narrow, succulent leaves taper upward and spread outward radially from a ground-level central stem. They feature toothed spines or threads along their edges and are tipped with a sharp-pointed terminal spine. Underground runners form new plants so they appear to grow in colonies. They store food in their thick leaves and upon reaching the age of 15 years or more, they shoot up a quick-growing stalk to as high as 20 feet. The stalks may be branched or unbranched and bear numerous white or pink flowers. These ultimately fruit a three-chambered cylindrical capsule containing many flat, black seeds. The following are some of the more common species.

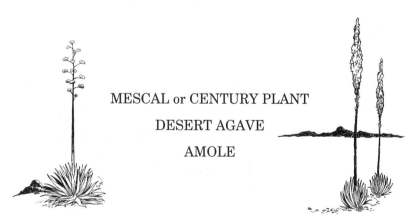

MESCAL or CENTURY PLANT

DESERT AGAVE

AMOLE

MESCAL or CENTURY PLANT
(Agave palmeri)

This is the largest native agave in the Southwest region. It usually appears solitarily, has thick green or blue-green leaves and flowers in June and July. Native Americans have traditionally derived mescal from it by baking the central stems. They also made ropes from the tough long fibers of its leaves. The Mescalero Apaches take their name from the use of Mescal as a food substance.

MESCAL or CENTURY PLANT

DESERT AGAVE
(Agave desertii)

This plant has narrow, widely-spread leaves, with toothed edges. It grows to 3500 feet in southern California and western Arizona and tends to flower in May. Native Americans bake the central stems in pits, making a gourmet food concoction.

DESERT AGAVE

AMOLE

(Agave lechuguilla)

This otherwise small specimen bears lavender-brown flowers in April and May on stalks which rise to heights of 25 feet. It ranges widely across the deserts of New Mexico, Texas and northern Mexico. The *lechuguilla* is to the Chihuahuan Desert what the Joshua Tree and Saguaro are to their locales. While it is poisonous to livestock, useful fibers are made from its leaves and a soap substitute called "amole" is derived from its short stem.

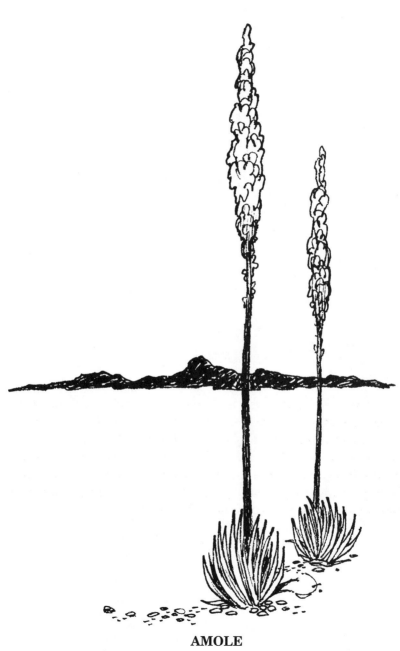

AMOLE

SOTOL

(Dasylirion wheeleri)

This round-headed plant features narrow, ribbon-like leaves to three feet in length which are split at the tips. Tiny flowers are creamy-colored and occur from May to August on a thin stem sometimes 15 feet tall. The base, stripped of leaves, provides food for livestock. A powerful beverage, Sotol, is derived from this good-looking plant's fermented sap. The Sotol is found primarily in the deserts of Arizona.

SOTOL

Bibliography

Benson, Lyman, *"The Cacti of Arizona"*
    The University of Arizona Press—Tucson, 1981

Benson, Lyman and Darrow, Robert, *"Trees and Shrubs of the Southwestern Deserts"*
    The University of Arizona Press—Tucson, 1981

Dodge, Natt N., *"Flowers of the Southwest Deserts"*
    Southwestern Monuments Assoc.—Globe, Arizona, 1965

Earle, W. Hubert , *"Cacti of the Southwest"*
    Desert Botanical Garden—Phoenix, 1966

Fischer, Pierre C., *"70 Common Cacti of the Southwest"*
    Southwest Parks and Monuments Assoc.—Tucson, 1989

Haustein, Erik, *"The Cactus Handbook"*
    Chartwell Books, Inc.—Secaucus, NJ, 1988

Hazelton, Scott E., *"Cacti for the Amateur"*
    Abbey Garden Press—Pasadena, 1958

Innes, Clive, *"The Handbook of Cacti and Succulents"*
    Chartwell Books, Inc.—Secaucus, NJ, 1988

Welles, Philip, *"Meet the Southwest Deserts"*
    Dale Stuart King—Tucson, 1964

CACTUS
Recipes

YUMMY!

Note: Laws on harvesting native desert plants vary by state. Before harvesting any native plants contact your local state agency.

Prickly Pear

The prickly pear cactus has the potential for becoming a tasty, inexpensive addition to our diets. Prickly pear cactus pads, commonly called nopales, can be used as a vegetable similar to green pepper or okra when properly prepared. They can also furnish important nutrients to the diet.

Often used in Shish-kabobs, pizzas, omelets and a variety of salads and casseroles it is also served plain with butter, tomatoes, rice or even made into a relish. In the spring, or after a rainfall, the younger small, dark green pads provide the tastiest options.

Prickly pear adds variety to any meal. All it takes is a little time and your own imagination.

In the fall, pick the fruit when it has attained the maximum redness for best flavor and color. Beware of stickers, wear heavy gloves and use metal tongs to handle the pears.

Flavors of prickly pears will differ. The sugar, acid and pectin of the fruit varies with its ripeness. For best results, prepare only small quantities at one time.

To remove stickers, here are some suggestions:

1) Brush pears with a vegetable brush.

2) Put fruit in a pan and pour hot water over it. This dissolves a film and stickers will fall off.

3) Wash pears with a spray hose to remove the spines and rinse.

4) Rub pears with a heavy cloth.

5) Singe pears over an outdoor grill.

Information and recipes furnished by the Cooperative Ex-
`n, University of Arizona, College of Agriculture. Addi-
`ecipes from *Cowboy Cartoon Cookbook* by Jim and Sue
`y and *Arizona Cook Book* by Al and Mildred Fischer,
√est Publishers.

Prickly Pear Cactus Jelly

3 cups **PRICKLY PEAR JUICE**
1/2 cup **LEMON JUICE**
1 pkg. **PECTIN**
4 1/2 cups **SUGAR**
1/2 tsp. **BUTTER**

To gather the prickly pears from the cactus, use a pail and long-handled tongs. (Collect approximately one gallon of pears.) When the pears are ripe, they will be a deep red color and will twist off easily. Pierce pears with a barbecue fork or use tongs, and place over hot fire on outdoor gas barbecue or fire source to remove bristles. They will require about one minute each over the fire. Then douse in cold water. Cut pears into on-inch chunks. Place in three-gallon pan (to allow foam to rise) with just enough water to cover. Bring to a low boil and cook for 30 minutes. Strain through colander and gently squash to remove remaining juice. Discard pulp. Pour juice through cheesecloth or fine woven strainer to remove any seeds or pulp. The juice is now ready to make jelly. If you wish to postpone, store juice in covered container in refrigerator up to 10 days.

Before you start, place jelly jars in dishwasher on hot cycle or boil according to direction.

Put juices (cactus and lemon) and pectin into a very large pan (at least three-gallon size). Dissolve pectin well with a whisk and bring to a boil, stirring constantly. Measure sugar into small bowl first, then add to pan, stirring constantly, and boil at a full rolling boil for two minutes. Turn off fire and add one-half teaspoon butter to eliminate any foam.

Pour into sterilized jars, wipe rim and seal. Yield: eight jars (8 oz. each).

Reprinted from *Cowboy Cartoon Cookbook*, by Jim and Sue Willoughby, Golden West Publishers.

Prickly Pear Puree

Force the raw fruit pulp through a food mill or a medium-fine wire strainer to remove seeds and heavy fibers. The puree may be packed into containers and frozen for future use. (Thaw before using in a recipe.)

Prickly Pear Salad Dressing

1/2 cup **PRICKLY PEAR PUREE**
1/3 cup **SALAD OIL** (not olive oil)
1 tsp. seasoned **SALT**
1 tsp. **SUGAR**
3 to 4 Tbsp. white wine **VINEGAR**

Shake all ingredients together in a covered jar or beat with a rotary beater. Makes about one cup of pink dressing. Serve on fruit or tossed green salads.

Prickly Pear Marmalade

4 cups chopped **PRICKLY PEARS**
1 cup sliced **LEMON**
2 **ORANGES**
SUGAR

Wash fruit and remove spines. Cut lemon into paper thin slices. Measure. Chop orange peel and pulp. Add 4 cups water to lemon and orange. Let stand 12 to 18 hours in a cool place. Boil until peel is tender. Cool. Pare, chop and measure pears. Measure lemon, orange and water in which cooked. Add 1 cup sugar for each cup pear, lemon, orange and water. Boil to jellying point. Pour, boiling hot, into hot jar; seal at once.

Prickly Pear Preserves

2 quarts **PRICKLY PEARS**
1 1/2 cups **SUGAR**
5/8 cup **WATER**
2 1/2 Tbsp. **LEMON JUICE**
1 slice of **ORANGE** (1/4 inch thick)

Prepare two quarts of prickly pear cactus fruit by removing the skins, cutting in halves, and removing the seeds. Cook the cactus fruit until transparent in a syrup made of the sugar, water, lemon juice and slice of orange. (Remove orange slice before packing preserves in jar.) Remove from heat and seal.

Prickly Pear Conserve with Rhubarb

1 cup **CACTUS** thinly sliced
1 cup **RHUBARB**, cut in pieces
2 slices of **PINEAPPLE**, thinly sliced
1/2 cup **PINEAPPLE JUICE**
1 1/2 cups **SUGAR**
1/2 **ORANGE**, juice and grated rind
1 1/2 doz. **DATES**, pitted and cut in pieces
1/3 cup **WALNUT MEATS**, broken in pieces

Combine all ingredients except the walnuts in saucepan and cook slowly until of desired consistency for conserve. Five minutes before removing from heat, add walnut meats.

Peeling a Prickly Pear

Cheese and Rice Topped Nopales

RICE FILLING

4 Tbsp. chopped **ONION**
1/2 lb. **HAMBURGER**
1 cup cooked **RICE**
3/4 cup **NOPALITOS**, parboiled and chopped
1/8 tsp. **OREGANO**
1/8 tsp. **PEPPER**

Brown hamburger. Add onion and cook until onion is soft. Add rice, nopalitos, and seasonings.

CHEESE SAUCE

2 Tbsp. **MARGARINE**
2 Tbsp. **FLOUR**
1 cup **MILK**
1 1/2 cups grated **AMERICAN CHEESE**
1 tsp. **SALT**
1/3 tsp. **PEPPER**

Melt margarine in saucepan and stir in flour. Slowly add milk, stirring continuously. Add spices and continue stirring until sauce is thick. Add cheese, and stir until melted.

NOPALE PADS

Parboil whole, young nopale pads (4 - 5) depending upon size. Add enough cheese sauce to the rice filling to hold it together. Pile this on top of the pads, top with cheese sauce, and bake in 350 degree oven to heat through.

Ensalada de Nopales

2 cups diced, cooked, chilled **NOPALES**
1 bunch, chopped **GREEN ONIONS**
2 **TOMATOES**, peeled and diced
2-3 **JALAPENOS**, chopped
1 4 oz. can **BLACK OLIVES**
1/4 cup **CILANTRO**
1/2 cup shredded **MONTEREY JACK CHEESE**

Marinate nopales in lemon juice at least one hour. Drain and mix with green onions, olives, jalapenos, tomatoes, and cilantro.

Arrange in serving dish on crisp lettuce and sprinkle cheese over all. Garnish with olives and serve cold.

Serves 8 (1/2 cup per serving).

Three Vegetable Salad and Dressing

1 cup **NOPALITOS**
1 cup **RED BELL PEPPER**
1/2 to 3/4 cup **ONION RINGS**, sliced very thin

Cut nopalitos and pepper in 1/4 by 1 inch strips and parboil.

DRESSING

1/2 cup **VINEGAR**
1/2 cup **VEGETABLE OIL**
1/2 cup **SUGAR**
1 tsp. **SALT**
1/2 tsp. **PEPPER**

Mix dressing in a blender or mixer until all sugar is thoroughly dissolved. Add the dressing to the vegetables in a bowl, cover and refrigerate. Salad will keep for several days.

Prickly Pear Pickles

2 qts. **PRICKLY PEARS**

SYRUP

2 cups **SUGAR**
2/3 cup **VINEGAR**
3 oz. **RED CINNAMON CANDIES** or **CLOVES** in
   cheesecloth bag

Remove skins from prickly pears, cut in halves, lengthwise.
Remove seeds. Cook until transparent in syrup. Remove spice
bag and can as any sweet pickle or preserve.

Nopalito Shish-Kabob

1/2 lb. **FLANK STEAK**, cubed and marinated in sauce below
8 **CHERRY TOMATOES**
1/2 cup chunked **PINEAPPLE**
1/2 cup chunked **NOPALITOS**, parboiled
8 fresh **MUSHROOMS**
8 small **WHITE ONIONS**, parboiled

On skewers, alternate the listed ingredients. Place over hot
coals or broil in oven until meat reaches desired doneness.
During cooking, baste kabobs with the marinade sauce.

MARINADE

1/4 clove **GARLIC**, minced
2 Tbsp. minced **ONION**
1/8 tsp. **OREGANO**
1/16 tsp. **THYME**
1/8 tsp. **PEPPER**
1/4 tsp. **SALT**
2 Tbsp. **VEGETABLE OIL**
4 tsp. **WHITE VINEGAR**

Combine ingredients, and add meat chunks. Let meat
marinate in sauce overnight in refrigerator.

Prickly Pear Cactus
Candy Cubes

2 qts. **CACTUS CUBES**

Remove spines and outside layer of cactus with a large knife. Cut pulp across in slices one-inch thick. Soak overnight in cold water. Remove from water, cut in one-inch cubes and cook in boiling water until tender. Drain.

SYRUP

3 cups granulated **SUGAR**
1 cup **WATER**
2 Tbsp. **ORANGE JUICE**
1 Tbsp. **LEMON JUICE**

Heat all ingredients until sugar is dissolved, then add cactus. Cook slowly in the syrup. Remove cactus, drain and roll in granulated or powdered sugar. For colored cactus candy, any vegetable coloring may be added to the syrup.

Three Day Cactus Candy

Cut cactus into one-inch slices. Take out the core and remove the rind, as only the pulp is used. Cube pulp and cover it with water. Boil for about 5 hours. Drain thoroughly. Make a solution that is 50 percent sugar and 50 percent white corn syrup. This mixture should cover the pulp. Cook pulp and syrup for an hour. Allow it to stand until the next day.

On the third day, cook syrup until it threads. It should look like preserves when ready to crystallize. Take another kettle and make a fresh mixture, using 2 parts sugar to 1 part corn syrup. Stir and cook this fresh mixture until it is a little cloudy. While still cloudy, take cactus pulp and drop each piece into mixture for about 2 minutes. (Several pieces may be dropped in at one time.) Remove with tongs and place on a piece of screen where it will drain. Do not put the pieces of cactus too close together as they will stick to each other.

Pepper Steak Nopale Style

1/2 lb. **FLANK STEAK** (use meat tenderizer if desired)
1/2 cup chopped **ONIONS**
1/4 cup **BEEF BROTH** or use bouillon
1 Tbsp. **SOY SAUCE**
1/2 clove **GARLIC**, minced
1/2 cup **NOPALE** strips
1 1/2 tsp. **CORN STARCH**
5 Tbsp. cold **WATER**
4 **CHERRY TOMATOES**, quartered

Brown meat. Add onions and cook until soft. Add broth, soy sauce, nopales, and garlic. Cover and simmer 10 minutes. Blend together corn starch and water, and add to meat mixture. Cook until thickened. Add tomatoes and cook until heated through.

Cactus Orange Marmalade

1/4 cup **ORANGE**, thinly sliced and cut in quarters
1/2 cup **ORANGE JUICE**
1 cup **CACTUS PULP,** thinly sliced
3/8 cup **SUGAR**

Cover orange with water and soak overnight. Add balance of ingredients and cook until it gives a satisfactory marmalade test.

Cactus and Apple Jelly

2 cups **CACTUS JUICE**
2 1/4 cups **SUGAR**
1 cup **APPLE JUICE**
PECTIN

Add small amount of pectin and bring to a fast boil, stirring constantly. Add sugar and bring to a hard boil (one you can't stir down with a spoon) and boil for 3 minutes. Remove from heat, skim and pour into hot canning jars leaving 1/4" headspace. Wipe jar rims and adjust lids. Process 10 minutes in a boiling water bath.

Cactus Pineapple Marmalade

1/4 cup **PINEAPPLE**, cut in thin slices (across rings)
1 cup **CACTUS PULP**, thinly sliced
3/8 cup **SUGAR**
1 to 2 tsp. **LEMON JUICE**, if desired

Cook until it gives a satisfactory marmalade test.

Cactus Juice Cocktail

1 pt. **CACTUS JUICE**   **LEMON JUICE**
1 pt. **CRANBERRY JUICE**   **WATER**
1 pt. **GINGER ALE**   **POWDERED SUGAR**

Mix first three juices. Dip rim of glasses in mixture of lemon juice and water then in sifted powdered sugar. Fill glasses with crushed ice. Pour cocktail over ice. Enjoy!

Saguaro Cactus Jam

8 lbs. **SAGUARO FRUIT**

Peel ripe fruit of Saguaro cactus using heavy gloves. Soak the fruit for about one hour. Drain enough liquid off the fruit so that the fruit is only half-covered with water. Boil for one-half hour. Strain off liquid, saving the pulp, and boil the liquid slowly to a syrup, stirring constantly as it burns easily. Crush the pulp and put through sieve to remove the seeds. Add the pulp to the thickened syrup and cook to consistency of jam. The jam is made without sugar as the fruit contains enough sweetening of its own.

Makes about three quarts of jam.

Saguaro Cactus Jelly

3 1/4 cups **JUICE** of **SAGUARO CACTUS FRUIT**

Gather the seedy centers of the ripe saguaro cactus fruit (no portion of hull or outside). The dried centers laying on the ground are all right, but some will have to be cut open and scooped out.

Place in a saucepan with about one inch of water above the centers. Simmer until cooked. Strain through a fine colander.

1 pkg. powdered **PECTIN**
1/4 cup **LEMON JUICE**
4 1/2 cups **SUGAR**

Put juice in a large kettle and add pectin and lemon juice. Stir to a full boil, then add sugar all at once. Bring to a boil, stirring constantly for one minute.

Pour into hot jars. Makes three pints of jelly.

About the Authors

Jim Willoughby trained in the Fine Arts at Pasadena City College and the Art Center School in California. Through the years he has drawn cartoons and written and illustrated articles for numerous national magazines. Presently he draws storyboards for various Hollywood animation studios. When not doing that or cooking up some exotic dish in the kitchen, he will most likely be found hiking with his granddaughters and dogs on the mountains surrounding the hilltop home he shares with his wife, Sue, in Prescott, Arizona.

His interest in cactus dates back to long-ago hitchhiking days. Just out of Ohio and traveling through the great Southwest he viewed his first towering Saguaros. Their majesty left him spellbound. A subsequent lifetime fascination with cacti and the study of them followed. It culminated in his collaboration with Sue in the writing and illustrating of this handy cactus handbook.

If Sue Willoughby wore hats she'd have a bunch. This is a gal on the run. In addition to writing books she is considerably involved with art and history-related community projects. Currently serving as Sheriff of the Prescott Corral of Westerners International, she also serves as Director of Prescott's Phippen Museum of Western Art and is active with the Prescott Art Docents, an affiliate of the Phoenix Art Museum. In what little time there is left to her, Sue enjoys being with and caring for her hillside gardens and many thriv-

ing house plants. You might correctly surmise that among these are an abundance of healthy, happy cacti specimens.

More Great Books from Golden West Publishers!

COWBOY CARTOON COOKBOOK

Zesty western recipes, cowboy cartoons and anecdotes. Cowboy artist Jim Willoughby and his wife, Sue, combined their many talents to produce these palate-pleasing selections. Saddle up the stove, 'cause you'll be riding the range tonight! *Cowboy Cartoon Cookbook* by Jim and Sue Willoughby (128 Pages) . . . **$5.95**

COWBOY COUNTRY CARTOONS

A cartoon excursion through the whimsical West of renowned cowboy cartoonist-sculptor-animator Jim Willoughby. Western humor at its ribald best! *Cowboy Country Cartoons* by Jim Willoughby (128 Pages) . . . **$4.50**

HIKING ARIZONA

50 hiking trails throughout this beautiful state. Desert safety—what to wear, what to take, what to do if lost. Each hike has a detailed map, hiking time, distance, difficulty, elevation, attractions, etc. Perfect for novice or experienced hikers. *Hiking Arizona* by Don R. Kiefer (160 Pages) . . . **$6.95**

ARIZONA OUTDOOR GUIDE

Guide to plants, animals, birds, rocks, minerals, geologic history, natural environments, landforms, resources, national forests and outdoor survival. Maps, photos, drawings, charts, index. *Arizona Outdoor Guide* by Ernest E. Snyder (128 Pages) . . . **$5.95**

More Great Books from Golden West Publishers!

GHOST TOWNS
and Historical Haunts in Arizona

Visit cities of Arizona's golden past, browse through many photographs of adobe ruins, old mines, cemeteries, ghost towns, cabins and castles! Come, step into Arizona's past! *Ghost Towns and Historical Haunts in Arizona* by prize-winning journalist Thelma Heatwole (144 Pages) . . . **$5.95**

EXPLORE ARIZONA!

Where to find old coins, bottles, fossil bed arrowheads, petroglyphs, waterfalls, ice caves cliff dwellings. Detailed maps to 59 Arizona wonders! *Explore Arizona!* By Rick Harris (128 Pages) . . . **$6.95**

DISCOVER ARIZONA!

Enjoy the thrill of discovery! Prehistoric ruins, caves, historic battlegrounds, fossil beds, arrowheads, waterfalls, rock crystals and semi-precious stones! *Discover Arizona!* By Rick Harris (112 Pages) . . . **$6.95**

SNAKES and other REPTILES
of the SOUTHWEST

This book is a must for hikers, hunters, campers and all outdoor enthusiasts! More than 80 photographs and illustrations in the text and full color plate insert, this book is the definitive, easy-to-use guide to Southwestern reptiles! *Snakes and other Reptiles* by Erik Stoops and Annette Wright (128 Pages) . . . **$9.95**

ORDER BLANK

Golden West Publishers

4113 N. Longview Ave.   •   Phoenix, AZ 85014

602-265-4392 • **1-800-658-5830** • FAX 602-279-6901

Number of Copies	TITLE	Per Copy	AMOUNT
	Arizona Adventure	5.95	
	Arizona Cook Book	5.95	
	Arizona Legends and Lore	5.95	
	Arizona Museums	9.95	
	Arizona Outdoor Guide	5.95	
	Cactus Country	6.95	
	Cowboy Cartoon Cookbook	5.95	
	Cowboy Country Cartoons	4.50	
	Cowboy Slang	5.95	
	Discover Arizona	6.95	
	Explore Arizona	6.95	
	Ghost Towns in Arizona	5.95	
	Hiking Arizona	6.95	
	Hiking Arizona II	6.95	
	Quest for the Dutchman's Gold	6.95	
	Snakes and other Reptiles of the SW	9.95	
	Wild West Characters	6.95	
Add $2.00 to total order for shipping & handling			$2.00

☐ My Check or Money Order Enclosed. . . . . $_____
☐ MasterCard   ☐ VISA

Acct. No.   Exp. Date

Signature

Name

Address

City/State/Zip

MasterCard and VISA Orders Accepted ($20 Minimum)
This order blank may be photo-copied.

4/93

Cactus Ctry